Embarrassment, Shame, and Guilt

CAUSES & EFFECTS OF EMOTIONS

CAUSES & EFFECTS OF EMOTIONS

Embarrassment, Shame, and Guilt

Kim Etingoff

Mason Crest

Mason Crest
450 Parkway Drive, Suite D
Broomall, PA 19008
www.masoncrest.com

Printed and bound in the United States of America.

First printing
9 8 7 6 5 4 3 2 1

Series ISBN: 978-1-4222-3067-1
ISBN: 978-1-4222-3069-5
ebook ISBN: 978-1-4222-8762-0

Library of Congress Cataloging-in-Publication Data

Etingoff, Kim.
  Embarrassment, shame, and guilt / Kim Etingoff.
     pages cm. — (Causes & effects of emotions)
  Audience: Grade 7 to 8.
  Includes index.
    ISBN 978-1-4222-3069-5 (hardback) — ISBN 978-1-4222-3067-1 (series) — ISBN 978-1-4222-8762-0 (ebook) 1. Embarrassment—Juvenile literature. 2. Shame—Juvenile literature. 3. Guilt—Juvenile literature. I. Title.
  BF575.E53.E85 2014
  152.4'4—dc23
                                              2014005463

CONTENTS

KEY ICONS TO LOOK FOR:

 Text-Dependent Questions: These questions send the reader back to the text for more careful attention to the evidence presented there.

 Words to Understand: These words with their easy-to-understand definitions will increase the reader's understanding of the text, while building vocabulary skills.

 Series Glossary of Key Terms: This back-of-the book glossary contains terminology used throughout this series. Words found here increase the reader's ability to read and comprehend higher-level books and articles in this field.

 Research Projects: Readers are pointed toward areas of further inquiry connected to each chapter. Suggestions are provided for projects that encourage deeper research and analysis.

 Sidebars: This boxed material within the main text allows readers to build knowledge, gain insights, explore possibilities, and broaden their perspectives by weaving together additional information to provide realistic and holistic perspectives.

INTRODUCTION

The journey of self-discovery for young adults can be a passage that includes times of introspection as well joyful experiences. It can also be a complicated route filled with confusing road signs and hazards along the way. The choices teens make will have lifelong impacts. From early romantic relationships to complex feelings of anxiousness, loneliness, and compassion, this series of books is designed specifically for young adults, tackling many of the challenges facing them as they navigate the social and emotional world around and within them. Each chapter explores the social emotional pitfalls and triumphs of young adults, using stories in which readers will see themselves reflected.

Adolescents encounter compound issues today in home, school, and community. Many young adults may feel ill equipped to identify and manage the broad range of emotions they experience as their minds and bodies change and grow. They face many adult problems without the knowledge and tools needed to find satisfactory solutions. Where do they fit in? Why are they afraid? Do others feel as lonely and lost as they do? How do they handle the emotions that can engulf them when a friend betrays them or they fail to make the grade? These are all important questions that young adults may face. Young adults need guidance to pilot their way through changing feelings that are influenced by peers, family relationships, and an ever-changing world. They need to know that they share common strengths and pressures with their peers. Realizing they are not alone with their questions can help them develop important attributes of resilience and hope.

The books in this series skillfully capture young people's everyday, real-life emotional journeys and provides practical and meaningful information that can offer hope to all who read them.

It covers topics that teens may be hesitant to discuss with others, giving them a context for their own feelings and relationships. It is an essential tool to help young adults understand themselves and their place in the world around them—and a valuable asset for teachers and counselors working to help young people become healthy, confident, and compassionate members of our society.

Cindy Croft, M.A.Ed
Director of the Center for Inclusive Child Care at Concordia University

Words to Understand

intense: Powerful; hard to resist.
negative: Having to do with or focusing on the downside of things.

ONE

WHAT ARE EMBARRASSMENT, SHAME, AND GUILT?

Gabriella was ready for the first day of school. She had new shoes. She had new notebooks and folders and pens.

She always liked the feeling of the first day of school—like this year would be better than all the other years. She would have more friends, better grades, and play better soccer. As Gabriella walked up the school steps, she knew she was ready for the school year.

Her very first class was science. She had a little trouble finding the classroom, so she got there just as the bell rang. The only open seat was by Cris, a boy she didn't know very well. She knew he liked to bully kids, so she was a little nervous about sitting next to him. She would have liked to sit next to her best friend Kati over on the other side of the room, but there was already someone sitting there.

Awkward moments happen to all of us—falling on our faces, burping at the wrong moments, and saying the wrong things.

Those oops moments make us wish we could push a button, rewind time, and do it all over again—only better this time.

Gabriella put her stuff down on the table and started to sit down. But instead of sitting in the chair, she felt herself falling! Before she really knew what was happening, she was sitting on the floor.

Everyone around her was laughing. Gabriella felt herself blush. She wished she were a million miles away, so no one could see her. She kept her eyes down and pulled the chair toward her. Class was about to start, so the only thing she could do was get up and sit on the chair. She was careful not to meet anyone's eyes. So much for a great school year.

Cris sat down in science class at a table near the back of the room. The rest of the tables filled up slowly, but no one sat next to him. He had hoped the new school year might be different, and that he might have more friends. It looked like this year was going to be like all the other ones.

EMBARRASSMENT, SHAME, AND GUILT

A bully may be trying to disguise his own insecurities by hurting someone else.

When we worry that we don't measure up in some way, it's sometimes easier to blame someone else.

Right before the bell rang, Gabriella walked in. He saw her look around and notice the empty chair next to him, which was the only one left. She frowned a little. Cris suddenly felt angry. Why didn't anyone want to sit next to him? Why was he stuck with the last person to come in to class?

Cris suddenly had an idea as Gabriella set her books down on the table. Right when she went to sit down, Cris whipped the chair out from under her. He pushed it back a few feet. He did it so fast Gabriella didn't even see it coming. Soon, she was sitting on the floor and everyone in class was laughing.

Cris thought bullying Gabriella would make him feel better. He wanted to feel like he was more powerful than other people. On the outside, he laughed with everyone else. Inside, he felt really, really bad. He didn't even know Gabriella very well. She hadn't really done anything to him. Why had he been mean to her?

When the teacher started talking, Cris couldn't pay attention. He was still feeling really bad. He felt bad for Gabriella, but he

Sometimes saying "I'm sorry" just doesn't seem like it's enough to make up for hurting someone.

also felt bad for himself. He couldn't get rid of the voice in his head that was saying awful things. The voice was saying, "No wonder you don't have any friends, you're mean and worthless. You deserve to sit alone and feel bad. You're always doing things wrong." Cris believed that voice.

Kati made it to science class early on the first day of school. She didn't want to be late and get in trouble on the very first day. She picked a seat near the front of the room and put her books on the table.

When Kati sat down, she tried to save a seat for her best friend Gabriella. She knew Gabriella was usually late for things, but maybe on the first day she would make it to class on time. No luck—Gabriella didn't show up until right before the bell, so Kati let another classmate sit next to her.

Kati watched Gabriella from across the room, trying to signal that she was sorry she couldn't save a seat for her. Gabriella didn't really notice, since she was trying to see if there were any empty seats left. Kati groaned as she realized her friend would have to sit next to Cris, the school bully.

Kati watched Cris as Gabriella sat down. She thought he might try something stupid. She recognized that look in Cris's eyes, which meant he was about to be mean. Sure enough, Kati saw him reach his hand out and pull the chair out from underneath Gabriella.

Kati felt really bad when she saw Gabriella on the floor and heard everyone laughing. She should have saved her a seat. She should have warned her about Cris before she sat down. She should have yelled a warning when Cris moved the chair back. She hadn't done any of those things, and now her best friend's day was ruined.

Gabriella, Cris, and Kati all experienced some bad feelings on their first day of school. However, each of them had slightly different feelings.

EMBARRASSMENT

Embarrassment is that I've-been-caught-with-my-pants-down feeling. It's not a pleasant feeling—but it goes away eventually.

Make Connections

No one agrees on how many emotions there are. Over the years, different thinkers and scientists have come up with different lists of emotions. Here are some of the different types of emotions in each category of emotion. Humans have a lot of feelings!

- anger: rage, irritation, jealousy, dislike
- disgust: revulsion, contempt
- fear: alarm, shock, horror, terror, nervousness, worry
- hope: expectancy, optimism
- joy: pride, contentment, cheerfulness, relief, excitement
- love: affection, attraction, infatuation
- sadness: despair, grief, disappointment, loneliness, guilt
- surprise: amazement, astonishment

Gabriella was embarrassed when she sat down on the floor in front of everyone in class. People were laughing at her. She blushed because she was embarrassed, and she couldn't look anyone in the eye.

Embarrassment is an emotion everyone has felt at one point or another. It's a normal, human emotion. We feel embarrassment when we're uncomfortable about something we've done in front of other people.

People feel embarrassed if they forget people's names when they're introducing them. They feel embarrassed if they trip on the stairs in front of other people. They're embarrassed if someone posts an awkward photo of them online.

Embarrassment is usually temporary. You feel embarrassed right after something happens—like tripping on the stairs—and then you forget it a little while later. You feel bad and uncomfortable, but embarrassment goes away.

Research Project

We use words to help us understand our emotions. Different words describe different "shades" of feeling. Using a thesaurus, either online or from the library, make a list of as many words as you can that relate to embarrassment, guilt, and shame. Use each word in a sentence in order to illustrate different shades of feeling.

Cris felt a different emotion called shame. Shame is when a person feels bad about doing something even if no one else has seen him do it. Other people might not know you are ashamed, but you definitely do.

Shame is more *intense*, and it makes you feel like you are a bad person or wrong or damaged. People who are ashamed blame themselves for being bad, and they feel like they are worthless. Shame can be a dangerous emotion if it goes on for too long or is too harsh.

Cris felt like he was a bad person for bullying Kati. He felt like no one wanted to be his friend because he was bad. Because he felt badly about his entire self, he was feeling shame.

Finally, Kati felt a third emotion that's related to embarrassment and shame. She was feeling guilty for not stopping Cris from hurting Gabrielle.

Guilt is the emotion a person feels when she feels bad about doing something specific. People feel guilty about cheating on tests or spreading rumors about a friend.

Guilt usually involves someone else. We feel guilty because our actions have hurt someone else. Kati felt guilty because she didn't save her friend a seat or stop Cris from bullying her.

Guilt is all about feeling bad about *doing* something specific. Unlike shame, guilt doesn't really make you feel like you are a bad person. You are just guilty you made a mistake.

Text-Dependent Questions

1. Explain what embarrassment is, using the story about Gabrielle as an example.

2. Define shame, using Cris as an example.

3. Describe guilt, referring to the story about Kati.

4. Explain how guilt and shame are different from each other.

Lots of people confuse guilt and shame, but they're different. Cris could have responded to his actions with guilt, not shame. If he felt guilty, he would just have felt bad that he pulled the chair out from under Gabrielle and maybe he wouldn't have done it again. Instead, he felt like what he did made him a terrible person who didn't deserve friends. That's shame.

All three of these emotions—embarrassment, shame, and guilt—are normal. People have lots of emotions, and **negative** emotions are just part of being human.

Understanding emotions helps you lead a better life. You'll have better relationships with your friends and family, you'll be happier, and you might even do better in school. Accepting emotions, even embarrassment, shame, and guilt, is a big part of growing up. The more you learn now, the better you'll be able to handle life!

Words to Understand

hardwired: Determined by our genes.
morally: Having to do with a person's or society's ideas of
   right and wrong.

TWO

YOU AND YOUR EMOTIONS

Feelings are a part of our everyday lives. They change pretty often. You might be feeling happy one minute, then remember a project you have to do for homework and get anxious. Then you might get excited while you're hanging out with friends, but angry when one of them says something with which you don't agree.

Every emotion has its own feeling. Your mind feels different with each emotion. Your body even does something different as it responds to each emotion. Embarrassment, shame, and guilt are all a little different once you get to know them.

EMOTION SCIENCE

Emotions are a huge part of being human. Just think what your life would be like if you never felt any emotions at all. You wouldn't

EMBARRASSMENT, SHAME, AND GUILT

Embarrassment can make your face get red and hot because brain chemicals are making your blood vessels a little bigger. This means that there is more blood just beneath the surface of your face's skin.

Make Connections

One of the big signs that someone is embarrassed is when her cheeks get red. Blushing is a physical response to embarrassment. We're the only species on Earth that blushes, and all of us do it! Embarrassment causes the body to release a chemical called adrenaline, the same chemical that causes you to run away or fight when you're scared or threatened. The body also releases adrenaline when you do something embarrassing. Adrenaline makes your heart race and your breath come faster. It also makes your blood vessels a little bigger. Mostly, you won't notice your blood vessels getting bigger—except in your face. Your skin is thin in your cheeks, so you can see all the blood flowing through the slightly bigger blood vessels. That blood is what causes blushing!

be happy on your birthday, you wouldn't feel sad if your friends were mean, and you wouldn't feel anxious when a big test was coming up.

Emotions are **hardwired** into our brains. There's no getting around them, even if you wanted to. Emotions have a lot to do with what's going on in our brains, which we then interpret as feelings.

Brains are made up of cells called neurons. Neurons send messages to each other, and eventually, they carry the messages to parts of your body outside the brain. Each neuron uses chemicals called neurotransmitters to send those messages. The chemicals travel between neurons, carrying the message with them. Millions of neurons are linked up together through neurotransmitters, which carry messages where they need to go.

Some of the messages those neurotransmitters carry are emotions. For example, a neurotransmitter called dopamine is involved

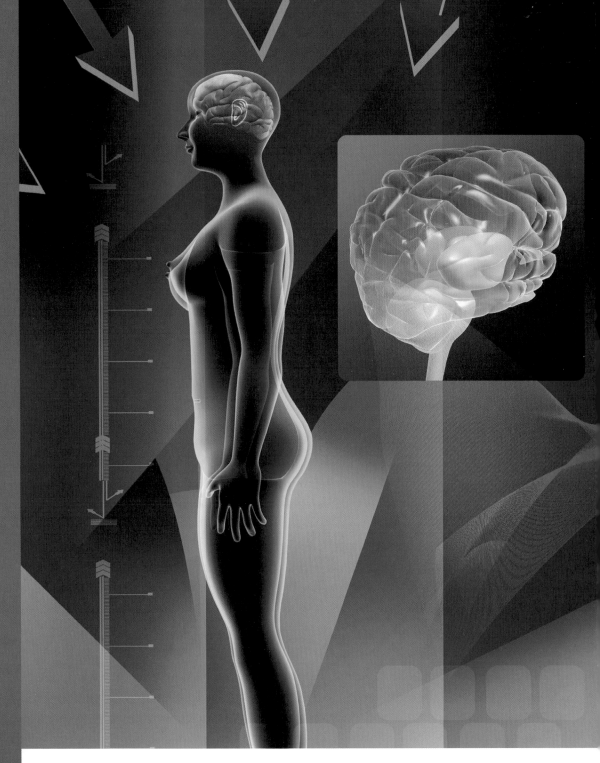

EMBARRASSMENT, SHAME, AND GUILT

The things going on in your brain have powerful effects on your entire body.

Make Connections

Emotions usually only last for a short period of time. Moods are something different. They last for days or weeks, and color everything you do during the day. You may feel angry for a little while after your friend tells you he doesn't like the clothes you're wearing. That's an emotion that will last for a few hours, and will come and go. If you didn't get much sleep last week, and you seem to be getting angry about every little thing that goes wrong, that's a mood. Your anger is lasting for a longer period of time than the angry emotion you felt because of your friend.

in happiness. When you do something pleasurable, like eat chocolate or hang out with friends, your brain releases dopamine. You interpret the feeling caused by that dopamine as happiness.

Emotions (and neurotransmitters) are reactions to what's going on in the world. They help us deal with both good and bad things that are happening to us. Emotions tell us some sort of change is happening, either out in the world or in ourselves. A scary change, like a huge thunderstorm rolling in, can trigger fear. A good change, like a friend telling you how much he appreciates you, can make you happy.

People tend to express their emotions with their bodies. Some people can hide their emotions, but most of us show some sort of emotion with our bodies. Facial expressions, where we look, posture, and how we move all tell other people how we're feeling. Showing emotions helps other people know how to deal with us, and it helps you know how to deal with others. If you can see your friend is upset, you can try and comfort her.

We all know what different emotions look like. We can even tell when someone else is feeling a familiar emotion. If someone

EMBARRASSMENT, SHAME, AND GUILT

Our faces reveal the wide range of our emotions.

Make Connections

 Researchers have come up with lists of the most common causes of embarrassment. Even just thinking about some of these things happening to you may make you feel a little embarrassed. You'll probably recognize some of them. You're not alone if anything on this list has ever happened to you!

• tripping and falling
• spilling a drink
• ripping your pants
• having someone tell others your secrets
• accidentally farting or burping
• getting too much attention paid to you, such as performing on stage
• forgetting people's names

is looking down, frowning, and sighing, you can quickly figure out that he's feeling frustrated or maybe sad. You definitely know he's not happy.

EMBARRASSMENT

Everybody feels embarrassed sometimes. We all do things we wish other people hadn't seen or heard about.

People feel embarrassed about all sorts of things. They feel embarrassed if they make a mistake, like accidentally putting on two different shoes and wearing them to school. They feel embarrassed if they can't control their bodies, such as letting out a huge burp in class. And people feel embarrassed if they do something unusual that most other people don't do. For example, you might be embarrassed if your friend told everyone you hate a movie that everyone else loves.

If you burp loudly while you're all alone, you're not likely to be embarrassed—but if you burp in the middle of an oral report in front of your entire class, it's a whole other story!

All those potentially embarrassing situations have some things in common. Another person has to be involved whenever you feel embarrassed. If you trip on the sidewalk and there's no one around to see you, you don't feel embarrassed—but you may feel embarrassed if you trip while walking with a group of your friends.

Someone has to see you for you to feel embarrassed, or you at least have to think someone has seen you. When you're embarrassed, you feel as though people are paying too much attention to you. You'd rather just go about your day without the extra attention. If just one person sees you do something embarrassing, you probably won't feel quite as bad as you would if ten people all see you do something embarrassing.

Your body reacts in certain ways when you get embarrassed. You don't just feel embarrassed—you look embarrassed. You blush and turn red in the face. You look down (usually to the left). You might also laugh nervously or try to hide your face with your hands. In Southeast Asia, people often bite their tongues when they're embarrassed.

SHAME

All sorts of things that happen in the world cause shame. Low grades at school could make you feel like you're stupid. Being rejected by friends or family can make you feel like you're not a worthwhile person. Anything that makes you feel like you are not good enough or something about you is wrong creates shame.

People often feel shame when they think they've done something *morally* wrong. In other words, we feel shame when we think we've been bad. We think we've made a serious mistake.

Shame tends to be more intense and long lasting than similar feelings like embarrassment. Shame sticks around for a while.

People can even feel shame if they haven't done anything wrong. They just have to think they have. A student might feel ashamed they got a B in a class, because the grade makes her feel stupid. But really, the class was hard, and no one is judging the student for getting a B. She hasn't done anything wrong, but she still feels ashamed.

Shame often involves feeling like you are "too" something. You may think you're too shy, too ugly, too stupid, too out of shape, or too talkative. On the other hand, you may also feel shame if you think you're "not enough" of something, like not smart enough, not interesting enough, or not athletic enough.

Different people experience different amounts of shame. Some people just naturally feel more shame than others—it's part of who they are. Many people who feel shame were told they weren't good enough when they were growing up. Their family or their friends criticized them and made them feel like they were bad in some way.

Like embarrassment, you feel and look a certain way when you're ashamed. You might have a hard time meeting anyone's eyes. You could feel anxious, which includes a fast heartbeat, a flushed face, and maybe even a stomachache.

Research Project

According to this chapter, people in Southeast Asia bite their tongues when they're embarrassed. Using the Internet or the library, find different ways people express emotions in different parts of the world. What body language is the same worldwide? What is different?

GUILT

Just like embarrassment and shame, everyone feels guilty from time to time. Guilt happens when we make mistakes, and everyone makes mistakes. It's good to feel guilty about them, so we can fix them and learn from them.

People often confuse guilt and shame. Guilt is a little different though. Guilt usually involves another person. We feel guilty when we hurt someone else. When someone feels guilty, he doesn't necessarily think that one mistake makes him a bad person. If he did think that, he would feel ashamed, not guilty.

Guilt involves doing something. You can feel guilty about spreading rumors about someone, or saying something mean to them. You can feel guilty about forgetting to feed the cat even though your family asked you to. You can feel guilty about letting your friend cheat off your test. In each case, you did something to feel guilty about. You've made a mistake.

Guilt tends to be a more temporary feeling than shame. You feel guilty right after you make a mistake. Then you might try to fix your mistake so you feel better. Even if you don't, guilt will fade away the farther you get from your mistake. The bigger the mistake, though, the greater guilt you're likely to feel and the longer it will last. Sometimes, guilt can turn into shame.

You can also feel guilty if you're just thinking about doing something but haven't done it yet. If you're thinking about cheating, or

Text-Dependent Questions

1. Explain what happens inside your body when you blush.

2. Explain what a neuron is and what it does.

3. According to this chapter, what are four ways that people can tell what we're feeling?

4. What is the difference between emotions and moods?

5. What is survivor's guilt?

spreading rumors, you can still feel guilty. The good news is that you haven't actually made the mistake yet!

Another common form of guilt is feeling guilty you didn't help someone. Kati felt this kind of guilt in the story in chapter 1. People feel guilty they haven't spent enough time with friends or family who are sick, that they haven't given enough money to help poor people, or they haven't volunteered enough at charities.

Yet another kind of guilt is called survivor's guilt. When someone outlives other people she cares about, she may feel guilty, even though she did nothing to cause the other person's death. Veterans coming back from war may feel guilt they survived even though some of their friends were killed in action. A person may feel guilty they are alive after a family member passes away from an illness or accident too.

Guilt is a hard emotion to feel. But guilt, like shame and embarrassment, can also help you. These emotions can help you get along better in life. If you work with them, they can help you become a kinder, better person.

Words to Understand

social: Having to do with the interactions between people.

positive: Having to do with or focusing on the good side of things.

researchers: Scientists who try to make new discoveries by doing experiments and collecting data.

participants: People who take part in something.

justified: Having a good reason to do something.

THREE

EMOTIONS AND LIFE

Emotions can take you on a daily roller coaster ride. You might start the day off angry when your little sister pokes you awake before you need to get up. As you're eating your favorite breakfast and watching TV, you're happy. When you trip on the bus stairs, you get embarrassed. And that's all before you even get to school!

Every day is filled with lots of emotions. Emotions have a purpose, and they happen for a reason. They help you figure out how you're feeling about your life and other people. Once you figure out your feelings, they can help you make changes that will make you better off in the long run.

EMOTIONS IN OUR DAILY LIVES

Emotions are useful. Without them, we'd be pretty lost and wouldn't know how to react to things that happen in the world.

EMBARRASSMENT, SHAME, AND GUILT

We interact with people in many ways every day. Our emotions help us respond to people and form relationships.

One big thing emotions do is help us form good relationships with other people. People are **social**. Throughout human history, for thousands and thousands of years, we've had to rely on other people to survive. Thousands of years ago, people couldn't survive if they couldn't hunt together or protect each other from wild animals. Today, we still need other people. We need them to grow our food, to make our clothes, and to build our houses.

We also need people to feel good about ourselves. If we don't have human contact, we quickly get sad. Contact with family, friends, and even strangers keeps us happy. Some people need more human contact than others, but we all need good relationships with family and friends to stay happy.

That's where emotions come in, including embarrassment, shame, and guilt. They tell us when relationships are going well, and when they need some work. They tell us when other people aren't treating us right, and when we aren't treating other people very well.

Emotions also tell us when we need to make changes in our lives. Negative emotions can be hard to deal with, but they're actually pretty useful. Maybe one group of friends you hang out with makes you feel bad all the time. You like having people to hang out with, but you don't like that they make fun of you. They make you do stuff you don't want to do, like skip class, and they tell you you're a loser when you don't want to do those things. Those friends aren't good for you, because they'll get you in trouble, and they aren't giving you respect.

You don't need anyone to tell you those friends aren't right for you if you pay attention to what your emotions are telling you. Your feelings are already sending you the message. You feel sad and sometimes angry whenever you spend time with those friends. Your negative emotions are telling you to stay away from them.

No one can be happy all the time. However, happiness and other **positive** emotions usually tell us when things are going right in our lives. If you feel happy hanging out with a certain group of friends, that's a good sign you've found the right people. Unlike

EMBARRASSMENT, SHAME, AND GUILT

If you always have a good time when you're with a group of friends, your emotions are letting you know that these are relationships you want to keep.

People who are sorry for their actions are showing that they think other people matter—and that's a good thing.

your other group of friends, these people make you feel good about yourself. They like to spend time doing the same things you like to do. Your positive emotions when you're around them are a clue you should keep these friends.

HELPFUL EMBARRASSMENT

Being embarrassed is actually a good thing. When someone is embarrassed, she realizes that she's made a mistake or has done something stupid. By showing embarrassment, she's showing other people she realizes she made a mistake. She's showing she knows other people are around.

And that's a good thing. People who are embarrassed realize other people matter. Imagine someone who never gets embarrassed. He doesn't really care what other people think. He might be mean or unfriendly. Other people don't really hang around

EMBARRASSMENT, SHAME, AND GUILT

If someone is sorry that he's hurt you and tries to make up for it, your relationship can become stronger in the end.

him because he doesn't care about his relationships much. He only cares about himself. That's an extreme example, but getting embarrassed shows other people you care about them and know they're looking at you.

Researchers have found that people who get embarrassed more easily are also more trustworthy and cooperate with other people better. Think about it—someone who is easily embarrassed cares about how other people think of them. When you care about other people, you're more likely to work with them well and be a good friend. You can definitely care too much about what other people think of you, but you should care a little!

In scientific studies, others see people who get embarrassed more often as being friendlier. They're seen as more trustworthy. In some studies, others were more likely to want to spend time with people who looked embarrassed in pictures, rather than people who looked proud. People actually like you more when you get embarrassed! Remember that the next time you feel yourself blushing.

GOOD GUILT

Guilt is another emotion that feels bad but is actually really helpful. If you never felt guilty after you hurt someone else, you might keep hurting other people. You wouldn't feel that pang of guilt that tells you that you did something wrong. Instead, you know to avoid that mistake in the future so you won't hurt anyone, and you won't feel guilty.

Guilt leads to good changes. Maybe you just told your friend a secret about another friend. You know you weren't supposed to tell anyone, since that's the point of a secret. The friend you told the secret to ends up blabbing it to a whole bunch of other people. Now your friend with the secret is really mad. You already felt a little guilty after you told the secret to one person. Now you feel really guilty! Your guilt teaches you to keep secrets from now on. You don't want to hurt anyone by telling secrets again, you

Gossip can seem like fun—you may not realize until later that you've hurt someone by talking about her behind her back. Guilt is the right thing to feel!

don't want to fight with your friends, and you don't want to feel so guilty. Guilt taught you an important lesson.

If you never felt guilt, you might keep hurting a lot of people in your life. Like embarrassment, the ability to feel guilt makes you more likeable and a better person. And other people know that too—if someone you hurt sees you're guilty about it, they're much more likely to forgive you.

Your friend whose secret you shared is really angry. You feel so guilty you go up to her and apologize. You tell her you know what you did was wrong, and you're not going to share anyone's secrets anymore because you realize what will happen if you do. If you're really sincere, your friend will probably forgive you, even if it takes her a little while. If you never felt guilty and you never told her you were sorry, she might stay mad at you for a long time. You could lose a friend.

Scientists have studied guilt to figure out just why we feel it, and how it helps us out. One study picked **participants** and gave them two choices of flavored jellybeans—fruit flavored and vomit flavored. Just about everybody chose the fruit flavored ones, for obvious reasons!

Then the researchers told the participants they would have to give the jellybeans they didn't eat to a partner they couldn't see. The researchers told them that rule was in the instructions they were given. Most people hadn't read the instructions fully, so they didn't know that was the rule. Now the participants who ate the fruit-flavored jellybeans felt guilty because their partners would have to eat the vomit flavored ones.

Then the participants played a special game. The researchers gave them $5 and told them they could keep some and give some to their same unseen partner. Participants who had eaten the fruit-flavored jellybeans gave their partners a lot more money because they felt guilty. They didn't even see their partners (who weren't real anyway), but even just thinking about making them eat vomit-flavored jelly beans made them guilty!

You can see that guilt is powerful—and that's a good thing.

We all want to feel accepted by the people around us. We don't want to feel that people don't like us—so most of us are willing to do a little work to make sure we have good relationships with others.

There's no point dwelling on something stupid that you did. The best thing is to learn from your mistake—and then move on.

Most of us want to have good relationships with people, even people we don't know. That makes the world a better place.

TOO MUCH

Emotions can go too far sometimes. When you feel the same emotion for a very long time, or feel an emotion really, really intensely, the emotion can become unhealthy.

Embarrassment, which is often a good thing, can become too much to handle. When you're feeling embarrassed, it can feel like the worst thing in the world. Then it fades as time goes on, and no one treats you any differently. No one remembers you did anything embarrassing. Everyone does embarrassing things!

Sometimes, though, you might replay the embarrassing scene in your head over and over again. You can't let it go, and you think everyone else must remember it too. You might be afraid to

EMBARRASSMENT, SHAME, AND GUILT

Teachers used to make students who made mistakes wear "dunce caps." The idea was that children could be shamed into performing better. Psychologists today believe that shame gets in the way of a healthy self-concept, making it very hard for a child to improve in school.

Make Connections

Researchers have found that embarrassment can have a dark side when it keeps us from doing something that would be good for us. They list the following actions when embarrassment can be a hindrance rather than a help: being too embarrassed to buy condoms, which could put people at risk of sexually transmitted diseases and unwanted pregnancies; being too embarrassed to get a health exam which could have detected a treatable disease; being too embarrassed to ask the teacher for help, and then doing badly on a test as a result.

go to school or hang out with friends because you think everyone is still secretly laughing at you. Embarrassment is meant to be a temporary emotion. When it becomes something you feel all the time, it gets in the way of your life.

Guilt can be the same way. Remember, guilt is a good thing to feel because it tells you when you need to be nicer to other people. Feeling too much guilt, though, isn't healthy.

Feeling guilty once in a while is okay. You should feel guilty if you forgot to feed your friend's pet fish while he was away for a weekend, or if you forget your grandma's birthday. Those are *justified* examples of guilt. You don't need to feel guilty for getting an A on a paper when your best friend got a B. That's not a good reason for guilt. Your guilt is unjustified.

Shame is one emotion that can be particularly hurtful to yourself and others. Most emotions are pretty temporary—they come and go throughout the day. Shame usually sticks around for a long time, which is a warning sign that too much shame can be unhealthy.

Shame gets in the way of feeling good about yourself. Feeling like you're a terrible person all the time isn't going to make life fun, and it isn't going to help you live your life to its fullest. Shame tells

Research Project

This chapter makes a connection between shame and drug and alcohol abuse. Use the Internet or the library to find a case study of someone who turned to drugs or alcohol as a way to handle shame. A case study is a report of a real-life situation, often written by a psychologist or a researcher. In your own words, write your own case study. Describe how shame affected the person's life. Was the person eventually able to overcome his or her shame? If so, what steps were taken?

you a lie about yourself: that you're not as good as others, that you're not valuable and special.

A little bit of shame can be okay. It can get you to make big changes that will make you feel better about yourself in the long run. For example, in the story in chapter 1, Cris felt ashamed that he bullied his classmate. He knew bullying is the wrong thing to do, and he felt bad about himself that he was a bully.

Cris is right that he shouldn't bully others, and feeling ashamed may help him decide to stop. If bullying makes him feel so bad about himself, he has a good reason to stop! As he treats people more kindly, he'll feel better about himself, and he won't be ashamed anymore.

But for a lot of people, shame doesn't lead to positive changes. Shame makes them feel worse and worse about themselves. They feel powerless to make any changes because they think they are such bad people.

Shame is particularly dangerous because it can lead to depression. Depression is a long-lasting feeling of sadness and hopelessness. People who are depressed find it hard to live life every day and do the things they used to enjoy. Shame and depression often go hand in hand.

Text-Dependent Questions

1. Explain the role emotions play in relationships.

2. Describe what scientists have discovered about embarrassment, according to this chapter.

3. In your own words, describe the findings related to guilt in the research study included in this chapter.

4. Explain how shame can be dangerous.

Shame may also lead to drug and alcohol abuse. Feeling bad about yourself all the time is very unhealthy, and it makes life a lot harder. Some people might turn to alcohol or drugs to make themselves feel better and ignore their shame for a while. Of course, alcohol and drugs will just create even more problems.

Ignoring your emotions just leads to trouble. Instead, you can learn from them.

Words to Understand

identify: Figure out what something is.

therapist: A person who helps people deal with and re-cover from emotional or mental problems.

strategies: Techniques or plans for how to deal with certain problems.

FOUR

LEARNING FROM YOUR EMOTIONS

Emotions are often confusing. They seem to make life a lot more complicated. A better way to look at emotions is to realize they make life more interesting! If you never felt any emotions, life would be pretty boring.

Of course, even though emotions are interesting and normal, that doesn't mean they make life easy. Learning how to *identify*, understand, and deal with your emotions is a big part of growing up. If you learn those skills, you'll be well prepared for the future. Emotions are a great way to learn about yourself, and to learn how to get along in the world.

IDENTIFY

The first step to learning from your emotions is to identify them. You have to know what you're feeling! Figuring out what you're feeling isn't necessarily easy. Some people can do it better than others, but everyone can learn to with practice. You may know

A journal can be a good tool for helping you to identify and understand your emotions.

you're feeling bad or good, but ask yourself if you can put a name to the emotion. How do you feel bad? You should also identify why you feel the way you do. What triggered your feeling?

Pay attention to your emotions through the day. Check in with yourself when you wake up. How do you feel? Then check in a few times later in the day. Do you feel differently from the way you did in the morning? Why or why not? You don't have to have all the answers. The idea is just to practice paying attention to your emotions and why you have them.

Putting your thoughts and feelings down on paper can help too. Make a list of your emotions throughout the day. Try to match them up with the things that make you feel that way. If you're taking a test, you might feel nervous, relieved, and then guilty. You feel nervous because you didn't study for the test, and you want to get a good grade to pass the class. You feel relieved when the test is over, because you don't have to worry about it anymore. You feel guilty, because you cheated on a couple questions by looking at your neighbor's test. You know cheating is wrong, and you're guilty because both you and your classmate could get in trouble.

You could also draw pictures to figure out your emotions. If something is bothering you, and you just can't figure it out, spend some time doing art or writing. You might surprise yourself by drawing or writing about the thing that's bothering you.

You'll get better and better at identifying your emotions as time goes on. Learning how to identify emotions comes as we age. When we're babies and little kids, we feel emotions, but we can't put words to them. Then we start learning about basic emotions, like happy and sad. As we get older, our emotions get more complicated, but we also learn how to talk about them to ourselves and to other people.

Embarrassment is usually a pretty easy emotion to identify. You do something in front of other people that you wish you hadn't, and then you feel embarrassed. If you're blushing and wish you could be miles away from the situation, chances are you're embarrassed!

Some emotions are too hard to handle by yourself. Counselors are trained to help you cope with your emotions.

Guilt is also fairly easy to identify. You feel a negative emotion after you hurt someone else. Sometimes, however, people hide their guilt from themselves. They don't want to face the fact they did something wrong and hurt somebody, so they bury their guilt.

Pay attention the next time you do something you know you're not supposed to do, or something that hurts somebody else. Do you feel bad? Are you avoiding talking to the person you hurt, or are you trying not to think about what you did? Those are good signs that somewhere inside, you feel guilty.

Shame is one of the harder emotions to identify. Shame definitely doesn't feel good, so you know something is going on if you feel ashamed! But people often confuse shame with guilt. Shame tends to last longer and feel more intense. It isn't necessarily tied to any single event, like guilt is. Shame is more about feeling bad about who you are.

If you're having trouble figuring out if you're feeling shame or guilt, ask yourself a few questions. Do you feel bad mostly about hurting another person, or do you feel bad about yourself? Do you feel bad about what you've done, or who you are? Have you felt bad for just a little while, or have you felt bad for a longer time? If you identify more with the second parts of these questions, you're probably feeling shame. Shame is harder to deal with by yourself. You may need to get some help from a counselor, *therapist*, or another adult who's trained to help.

ACCEPT

Once you can identify your emotions and why you feel them, you can focus on accepting them. Just about everybody has trouble sometimes accepting their emotions. When you feel bad, it's hard to tell yourself that it's okay that you're feeling bad instead of just immediately trying to avoid the feeling.

Accepting isn't the same as giving in to your emotions. Accepting an emotion is recognizing that you're feeling it, and telling yourself it's okay you're feeling it. You need to give yourself time to feel, and then time to decide how to deal with the emotion.

You should always remind yourself that feeling emotions is a normal part of being a person. In fact, you can do a lot of damage if you don't let yourself feel emotions. Don't judge yourself for feeling a certain way at a certain time. Whatever you're feeling is what is happening at the moment. You just need to decide how to deal with the emotion you're feeling.

Think of a young person who bottles up a lot of anger inside. He doesn't want to feel angry, because it isn't a pleasant feeling. He thinks he should be happy all the time, and that feeling anger is bad. Bottling all that anger up works for a little while. But then his friend teases him a little, as a joke. Instead of just telling his friend to stop because the teasing is hurting his feelings, he blows up. He yells and maybe even physically hurts his friend, as all that bottled anger comes out all at once. The young man could maybe have avoided that extreme response if he has just accepted his anger at first and found a healthy way to express it.

Always remember that your feelings are temporary. Even if you feel really, really bad, you'll feel good again sometime soon. Even the worst negative feelings will go away eventually.

Accepting embarrassment, shame, or guilt is pretty hard! Instead of acceptance, you probably just want to forget you feel so bad. You'll be much better off, though, if you deal with these emotions now, and learn to accept them. Whenever you find yourself feeling embarrassment, shame, or guilt, let yourself. Don't immediately push the emotion away or try to hide from it.

Instead, think about the feeling. Why do you feel guilty? What did you do to feel guilty? When you do the work of accepting your feelings, you can start to learn from them.

REFLECT AND LEARN

Remember that your emotions happen for a reason. Try to figure out what message your emotions are trying to tell you, and then pay attention!

Guilt is a powerful way to learn about what's right and wrong. You know when you do something wrong. And when you feel so bad after you do it, you're more likely to avoid hurting others in the future. Whenever you feel guilty, your mind is telling you to do something different.

People can tell you not to tease others, not to steal, or not to skip class. For some people, though, guilt is a better teacher than anyone telling them what to do or not do. The guilt you would feel after teasing, stealing, or skipping class would really teach you a lesson.

You can learn a lot from shame too, in small doses. Shame can

Make Connections

For some people, negative emotions aren't temporary. They become permanent, and take over their lives, hurting them and other people. If you feel really negative emotions all the time, you don't have to accept that. If you think your emotions might be unhealthy, or you need help with anger or extreme sadness, or someone is making you feel bad all the time, there are people to turn to for help. Guidance counselors and psychologists at school are there to help students through difficult problems, including problems with emotions. Therapists and social workers outside of school are also trained to help young people with problems. If your emotions are taking control of your life, consider getting some help. You'll learn new ways to think and some tricks for taking back control.

tell you when you're unhappy with the way you're doing things in general.

You need to be careful to learn from shame in a healthy, positive way. Let's say you're ashamed you're not athletic enough. Everyone else is on a sports team, they can run miles and miles, and they all look fit. An unhealthy response to the shame would be to do nothing and continue to feel badly about yourself all the time. Another unhealthy response would be to exercise so much you get sick.

Healthier responses include making some small changes. Find an exercise program that's right for you or find a sport you like. Make some friends who encourage you to exercise. Meanwhile, work on learning to love yourself as you are, not as you think you should be. Handled this way, should could help you become a healthier, happier person.

One of the best ways to learn from your emotions is to talk to other people about them. Getting someone else's point of view on what you're feeling may help you understand some things you didn't before. And when you have to use words to describe your emotions and why you're feeling them, you'll learn more too.

Talking about feelings is hard for a lot of people. The first time you do it won't necessarily be easy. Choose who you talk to carefully. Talk to a trusted friend who is good at listening. Talk to your parents or a family member you trust. Talk to an adult at school, like a teacher or guidance counselor, who can offer really good advice. You'll be surprised at how much better you feel after talking! You'll also have better relationships with the people you talk to, because you're showing them you trust them.

Talking about embarrassment, shame, and guilt makes them a little less horrible. It's almost like you're getting rid of the emotions as you talk about them. The person you're talking to can also help you learn from your emotions, rather than just feel badly about them.

TAKE CHARGE

Emotions don't need to take over your life. Once you accept whatever emotion you're feeling, you can then take charge over it.

Taking charge over your emotions involves finding healthy ways of expressing them. Yelling at and fighting a friend is not a healthy way of dealing with anger. Taking out anger by exercising or doing a sport and then calmly talking to your friend about why you are mad is a much healthier way of dealing with your anger.

Take embarrassment, for example. You will definitely find yourself in many embarrassing situations during your life, simply because you're human. But there are plenty of **strategies** for dealing with embarrassment, to help you deal with it and not let it rule your life.

Imagine you just did something really embarrassing. Maybe you just spilled your drink all over the lunch table. Everyone is laughing and you feel yourself blushing. You're having trouble breathing normally because you're so embarrassed.

Luckily, you can calm down. Focus on breathing deeply and

Make Connections

Negative emotions happen, but you don't have to let them take over your life. If you want to feel better, try out some of these things:

- Exercise. Moving and exercise gets your brain to release chemicals that make you feel better. You can do any exercise you like—run, swim, take a hike, dance, jump on a trampoline. All of them will get you feeling better!
- Focus on thinking positively. Pay attention the next time you feel bad—you're probably thinking pretty negatively. Instead of thinking bad things about yourself and what's going on, focus on all the good things. Make a list of what you're thankful for, or what you like about yourself or your life. Practice thinking positively whenever you can.
- Eat healthy. Eating junk food all the time can make you feel worse. Lots of people eat junk food when they're unhappy, but the opposite will work a lot better. Junk food makes you feel tired, run down, and cranky. Healthy food gives you energy and makes your body work better.
- Do art. Write a poem, paint a picture, or play some music. Art helps you release and express your emotions in a healthy way. Instead of blowing up in anger at someone, you should try writing a poem or drawing how you feel.

slowly. Your heart will stop pounding so much, and your blush will go away. You can also try and get people to stop paying attention to you. Change the subject, or remind everyone about what they were talking about right before you spilled your drink.

The best thing to do when you get embarrassed is to laugh about it. If someone else had spilled her drink, you would be laughing. So why shouldn't you laugh at yourself? If you can see

EMBARRASSMENT, SHAME, AND GUILT

Research Project

The sidebar on page 57 indicates that there's a connection between emotions and diet. Use the Internet and the library to investigate this connection further. List the five food groups and explain how each contributes in some way to emotional health.

the humor in the situation, you can see that your embarrassment isn't really a big deal.

Dealing with guilt is also pretty straightforward, but it's often hard to do. When people feel guilt about something, they usually want to fix it. After spreading a rumor about a friend, you can apologize. After getting a bad grade because you goofed off, you can work extra hard.

If people can't directly make up for what they've done to someone, they can help somebody else out to make themselves less guilty. Maybe you're feeling guilty you didn't see your grandfather as much as you should have before he died, so you make up for it by spending more time with the rest of your family. Or maybe you go visit other elderly people in a nursing home.

Shame is a harder emotion to learn how to control. When you're ashamed, you feel like something is wrong with you. You have a couple choices after you recognize you're ashamed. You can try to make the shame go away because it's not based on reality. Or you can choose to accept your shame and then work to change yourself and become a better person. In either case, you may need help from someone else so that you can take charge of your shame rather than allowing it to control you.

Thinking about emotions as learning tools is a big change from how most of us think about them. Learn what your emotions are, including embarrassment, shame, and guilt. Figure out why you

Text-Dependent Questions

1. What does this chapter suggest as methods for helping you identify your emotions?

2. What role does acceptance play in handling our emotions, according to this chapter?

3. When does the author say people should get help with their emotions?

4. What examples does this chapter give of ways a person might learn from guilt?

5. Explain how you can take charge of emotions, according to this chapter.

6. What four methods does the sidebar list for feeling better emotionally?

feel them. Then accept those feelings, even if they're awful. Use them to learn about what you need to change in your life! Finally, take charge and make those changes. Let your emotions happen, but be in charge.

All of this takes practice. Take time to think about embarrassment, shame, guilt, and the whole range of other emotions. Practice dealing with them and it will get easier with time. No one is ever perfect at managing emotions, but we can all work to get better—and we will.

Find Out More

IN BOOKS

Andrews, Linda Wasmer. *Emotional Intelligence.* New York: Scholastic, 2004.

Hamil, Sara. *My Feeling Better Workbook: Help for Kids Who Are Sad and Depressed.* Oakland, Calif.: New Harbinger Publications, 2008.

Morrison, Betsy S. *Self-Esteem.* New York: Rosen Publishing, 2011.

Shaw, Tucker. *What's That Smell? Oh, It's Me: 50 Mortifying Situations and How to Deal.* London, U.K.: Puffin, 2003.

Spilsbury, Richard. *Emotions: From Birth to Old Age.* Portsmouth, N.H.: Heinemann, 2013.

ONLINE

KidsHealth: Talking About Your Feelings
kidshealth.org/kid/feeling/thought/talk_feelings.html

KidsHealth: Understanding Your Emotions
kidshealth.org/teen/your_mind/emotions/understand-emotions.html

Palto Alto Medical Foundation: Emotions and Life
www.pamf.org/teen/life

PBS Kids GO!: Embarrassing Moments
pbskids.org/itsmylife/school/embarrassing/article3.html

Series Glossary of Key Terms

adrenaline: An important body chemical that helps prepare your body for danger. Too much adrenaline can also cause stress and anxiety.

amygdala: An almond-shaped area within the brain where the flight-or-flight response takes place.

autonomic nervous system: The part of your nervous system that works without your conscious control, regulating body functions such as heartbeat, breathing, and digestion.

cognitive: Having to do with thinking and conscious mental activities.

cortex: The area of your brain where rational thinking takes place.

dopamine: A brain chemical that gives pleasure as a reward for certain activities.

endorphins: Brain chemicals that create feelings of happiness.

fight-or-flight response: Your brain's reaction to danger, which sends out messages to the rest of the body, getting it ready to either run away or fight.

hippocampus: Part of the brain's limbic system that plays an important role in memory.

hypothalamus: The brain structure that gets messages out to your body's autonomic nervous system, preparing it to face danger.

limbic system: The part of the brain where emotions are processed.

neurons: Nerve cells found in the brain, spinal cord, and throughout the body.

neurotransmitters: Chemicals that carry messages across the tiny gaps between nerve cells.

serotonin: A neurotransmitter that plays a role in happiness and depression.

stress: This feeling that life is just too much to handle can be triggered by anything that poses a threat to our well-being, including emotions, external events, and physical illnesses.

Index

Picture Credits

63

About the Author & Consultant

Kim Etingoff lives in Boston, Massachusetts. She spends part of her time working on farms, and enjoys writing on topics related to health and wellness.

Cindy Croft is director of the Center for Inclusive Child Care at Concordia University, St. Paul, Minnesota where she also serves as faculty in the College of Education. She is field faculty at the University of Minnesota Center for Early Education and Development program and teaches for the Minnesota on-line Eager To Learn program. She has her M.A. in education with early childhood emphasis. She has authored *The Six Keys: Strategies for Promoting Children's Mental Health in Early Childhood Programs* and co-authored *Children and Challenging Behavior: Making Inclusion Work* with Deborah Hewitt. She has worked in the early childhood field for the past twenty years.